D0603902

Dinosaur Detectives
Search for the Facts...

Placodus
and Other
Swimming Reptiles

Tracey Kelly

BROWN BEAR BOOKS

Published by Brown Bear Books Ltd
4877 N. Circulo Bujia
Tucson, AZ 85718
USA

and

Leroy House
436 Essex Rd
London N1 3QP
UK

ISBN 978-1-78121-409-1

Library of Congress Cataloging-in-Publication Data available on request

Text: Tracey Kelly
Designer: John Woolford
Design Manager: Keith Davis
Editorial Director: Lindsey Lowe
Children's Publisher: Anne O'Daly
Picture Manager: Sophie Mortimer

Picture Credits
Public Domain: G. hedoghedo/Staatliches Museum Stuttgart 4.

Brown Bear Books has made every attempt to contact the copyright holder.
If you have any information, please contact: licensing@brownbearbooks.co.uk

Manufactured in the United States of America
CPSIA compliance information: Batch#AG/5609

Websites
The website addresses in this book were valid at the time of going to press. However, it is possible that contents or addresses may change following publication of this book. No responsibility for any such changes can be accepted by the author or the publisher. Readers should be supervised when they access the Internet.

Contents

How Do We Know about Dinosaurs?

Scientists are like detectives.

They look at dinosaur fossils.

Fossils tell us where dinosaurs lived.

They tell us how big they were.

This skeleton is *Placodus*.
It is a swimming reptile.
It is 240 million years old.
You might see one in
a museum!

How to Use This Book

This tells you what the animal ate.

🌿 Plant-eater

🦎 Meat-eater

This tells you when the animal lived.

240 million years ago

SWIMMING REPTILES

Placodus

Say it! (PLAK-oh-duss)

Placodus was not a good swimmer!
It had a chunky body and a short head.
Placodus walked slowly on the shore.
It grabbed shellfish off rocks.

MINI FACTS
Placodus had strong teeth. They could crunch shellfish.

Strong legs

Clawed feet

Swishing tail for balance

Heavy body

FACT FILE
NAME: *Placodus* means "flat tooth"
WEIGHT: about 440 pounds (200 kg)
FOOD: shellfish
HABITAT: shallow waters near coasts

How big am I?
6 ft (2 m)

First found in — France, 1833

18

19

This shows you how big the animal was.

A map shows where the first fossils were found.

Read on to become a dinosaur detective!

5

Swimming Reptiles

Large reptiles swam in the ocean.
Smaller reptiles swam in ponds and rivers.
They lived from 300 million years ago to 66 million
years ago. Some had paddles to help them swim.
Some had strong legs. They could crawl
across land. They hunted fish and animals.

Champsosaurus

Say it! **(KAMP-so-SAW-rus)**

Champsosaurus looked like a crocodile.
It had a long jaw full of teeth. It lay
at the bottom of ponds and grabbed fish.

Strong jaws with sharp teeth

Strong neck

KENNEDY

Legs stuck out to the sides

⚡ MINI FACTS

The females laid their eggs on land. Males stayed in the water.

FACT FILE

NAME: *Champsosaurus* means "crocodile reptile"

WEIGHT: 60 pounds (27 kg)

FOOD: fish

HABITAT: rivers and swamps

Strong tail with narrow tip

How big am I?

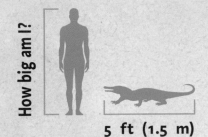

5 ft (1.5 m)

First found in ...
North America, 1876

Ichthyosaur

Say it! (ICK-thee-oh-SORE)

Ichthyosaurs were sea reptiles. They looked like dolphins. Some were big. Some were small. They ate fish and sea creatures.

Strong tail for swimming

MINI FACTS

Ichthyosaurs did not lay eggs. They gave birth to live babies!

How big am I?
1–69 ft (0.3–21 m)

FACT FILE

NAME: ichthyosaur means "fish lizard"

WEIGHT: up to 30 tons
(up to 27 metric tons)

FOOD: fish, squid, and small sea creatures

HABITAT: the ocean

Fin helped
steering

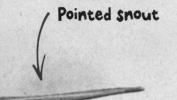
Pointed snout

Flippers

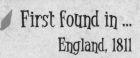
First found in ...
England, 1811

11

Kronosaurus

Say it! (CROW-no-SAW-rus)

Kronosaurus was a large reptile. It had a big head. It had four paddles. *Kronosaurus* ate fish and squid. It ate turtles, too.

Large head

Sharp teeth

Powerful front flippers

MINI FACTS

Kronosaurus could eat almost anything. Its teeth were as big as bananas!

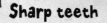

How big am I?

33 ft (10 m)

FACT FILE

NAME: *Kronosaurus* means "Kronos lizard"

WEIGHT: 10 tons (9 metric tons)

FOOD: large fish, squid, turtles, and other swimming reptiles

HABITAT: the ocean

Tail helped steer animal

Paddles for swimming

First found in ...
Australia, 1899

13

Liopleurodon

Say it! (LIE-oh-PLOO-ro-don)

Liopleurodon was large. It had a long snout. It had sharp teeth. This reptile swam very fast! It chased large sea animals.

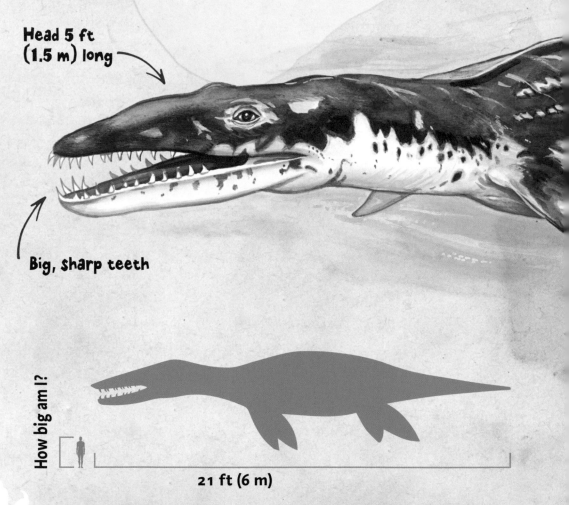

Head 5 ft
(1.5 m) long

Big, sharp teeth

How big am I?

21 ft (6 m)

FACT FILE

NAME: *Liopleurodon* means "smooth-sided tooth"

WEIGHT: 1.8 tons (1.7 metric tons)

FOOD: fish and other sea animals

HABITAT: the ocean

Long body and short tail

MINI FACTS

Liopleurodon ate lots of food. It mostly ate fish.

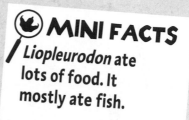

Flippers for fast swimming

First found in ...
France

Peloneustes

Say it! (PEL-oh-NEW-steez)

Peloneustes was the size of a dolphin.

It had a large head and a short neck.

Peloneustes was a fast swimmer.

It hunted squid and small prey to eat.

⚲ MINI FACTS

Peloneustes had a narrow mouth. It could only eat small creatures.

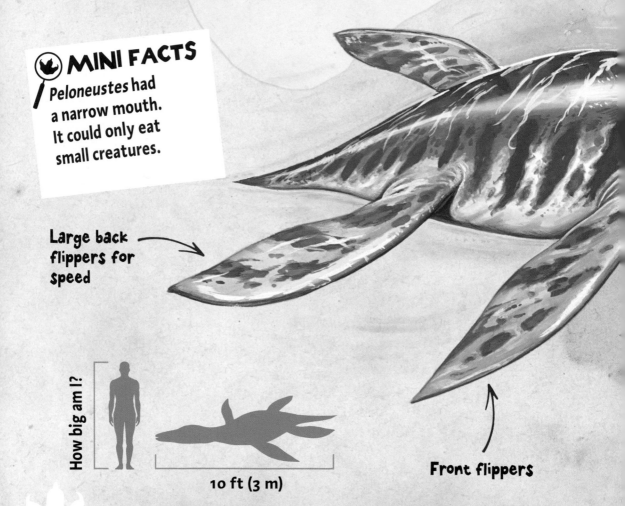

Large back flippers for speed

Front flippers

How big am I?

10 ft (3 m)

FACT FILE

NAME: *Peloneustes* means "mud swimmer"
WEIGHT: 660 pounds (300 kg)
FOOD: fish, squid, and shellfish
HABITAT: shallow seas

Long snout and
sharp teeth

Short neck

First found in ...
England, 1869

Placodus

(Say it!) (PLAK-oh-duss)

Placodus was not a good swimmer!
It had a chunky body and a short head.
Placodus walked slowly on the shore.
It grabbed shellfish off rocks.

MINI FACTS

Placodus had strong teeth. They could crunch shellfish.

Strong legs

Clawed feet

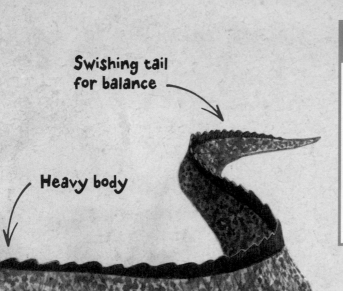

Swishing tail for balance

Heavy body

FACT FILE

NAME: *Placodus* means "flat tooth"

WEIGHT: about 440 pounds (200 kg)

FOOD: shellfish

HABITAT: shallow waters near coasts

How big am I?

6 ft (2 m)

First found in ...
France, 1833

Plesiosaurus

Say it! (PLES-ee-oh-SORE-us)

Plesiosaurus lived in the ocean.
But it came up to breathe air!
It chased prey and grabbed it
with curved teeth.

Long, bendy neck

Small head with
pointed snout

How big am I?

Paddles for
swimming

10 ft (3 m)

FACT FILE

NAME: *Plesiosaurus* means "nearly a lizard"

WEIGHT: about half a ton (454 kg)

FOOD: fish, squid, and small animals

HABITAT: shallow oceans and seas; laid eggs on sandy beaches

⊛ MINI FACTS

Plesiosaurus came onto beaches to lay its eggs. Sea turtles do this today.

Short, wide body

First found in ...
England, 1823

Short tail

21

Dinosaur Quiz

Test your dinosaur detective skills!
Can you answer these questions?
Look in the book for clues.
The answers are on page 24.

2 Which reptile was the size of a dolphin?

Which reptile grabbed shellfish off rocks?

1

Which reptile looked like a crocodile?

3

4 Which animal had a long, bendy neck?

Glossary

fossil

Part of an animal or plant in rock.
The animal or plant lived in ancient times.

habitat

The kind of place where an animal
usually lives.

paddles

Limbs that help a reptile
swim underwater.

prey

An animal that is hunted
by other animals for food.

Find out More

Books

National Geographic Little Kids First Big Book of Dinosaurs, Catherine D. Hughes (National Geographic Kids, 2011)

The Usborne Big Book of Dinosaurs, Alex Frith, (Usborne, 2017)

Websites

discoverykids.com/category/dinosaurs/

www.kidsdinos.com/dinosaurs-for-kids/

www.kids-dinosaurs.com/swimming-dinosaurs.html

Index

Quiz Answers: 1. *Placodus* grabbed shellfish off rocks. **2.** *Peloneustes* was the size of a dolphin. **3.** *Champsosarus* looked like a crocodile. **4.** *Plesiosaurus.*